START WHERE
YOU FIND
YOURSELF

START WHERE YOU FIND YOURSELF

Lessons Taught and Lessons Learned

BY

Charlie Nelms, Ed. D.

ISBN: 0-9616649-1-6

PUBLISHED BY SABAYT PUBLICATIONS

FOR ADDITIONAL COPIES, PLEASE WRITE TO:

PO BOX 6544

BLOOMINGTON, INDIANA 47407

OR

PLANTATIONS03@HOTMAIL.COM

It ain't nothing to find no starting place in the world. You just start from where you find yourself.

August Wilson in *Joe Turner's Come and Gone*

For Jeanetta Sherrod Nelms and
Rashad Z. Nelms, my spouse, son, and best
supporters, who have teamed with me to leave
the world better than we found it.

For Mama and Papa who always encouraged us
to pursue our dreams with passion and
persistence no matter the obstacles.

For the teachers and counselors from all
walks of life who encouraged me when I was
down, celebrated my success when I was up,
and implored me to always remain
true to myself.

CONTENTS

ACKNOWLEDGMENTS

This project would not have been completed without the expert assistance of Janet Cheatham Bell of Publishing Consulting Services and Storme Day from Indiana University. I am likewise grateful to the countless friends, colleagues, and students who have inspired me over the years.

PREFACE

As a child growing up in the Delta Region of Arkansas, I wish I could say that my motivation for doing well in school was fueled by some inherent desire to succeed, but it wasn't. It was fueled by my determination to escape our leaky tin roof house, the sun-up to sun-down days in the cotton field, the outhouse, coal oil lamps, and the other evils of poverty and racism. It was there, in the cotton fields, that I learned to dream and to strategize about how to help myself and to change the world. My body was in the cotton fields, but my mind was never there.

Although my parents were barely literate, they instilled in my ten siblings and me an abiding faith in education as a vehicle for personal, economic, and social change. This faith in education was proclaimed by preachers, professed by parents, and reinforced by teachers, and 4-H club leaders.

This collection of original quotes is a reflection of some of my most intimate thoughts; they reflect the lessons about a variety of important topics that others have taught me or that I have sought to teach others. They represent thoughts that I have scribbled on scraps of paper while listening to my inner voice and they represent thoughts I have included in my speeches around the world.

In keeping with my desire to leave the world better than I found it, I share them in this little book with the hope they will inspire and provoke others to act.

Charlie Nelms

INTRODUCTION

Everyone has his or her own sense of what a collection of quotes represents. In my mind, a volume of this sort falls somewhere between being the literary representation of a bottle of vitamins and a box of chocolates. You get to pick whatever confection most suits your taste at the moment, with the understanding that while your selection is probably not going to change your life, it does have the potential to help you be a bit more uplifted as you go about whatever it is that you're doing.

Charlie Nelms has done his readers a service by putting together a collection of statements, phrases, and observations that bring us to a pause as we consider and savor the messages. This volume contains a wide variety of short, thoughtful, sayings - some of which can be interpreted in an intensely personal way, and others in a manner that is reflective of the general human condition.

What's the best testimony that a book of quotes has met its goal? For me, it's whether the quotes still ring in your consciousness after you've closed the book and gone on to do other things. I think you'll find that to be true of this volume.

The quality of reflection has become nearly a lost art in this frenetic world that we inhabit. With this volume, Charlie Nelms gives us a useful tool to reposition that element into our lives. We owe him our thanks for doing so.

WILLIAM B. HARVEY
VICE PRESIDENT AND DIRECTOR
OFFICE OF MINORITIES IN HIGHER EDUCATION
AMERICAN COUNCIL ON EDUCATION

START WHERE
YOU FIND
YOURSELF

INSPIRATION
AND
ENCOURAGEMENT

The stars shine even on the darkest nights.

*Vision without focus is a
mere illusion.*

*No matter how dreary, there is
beauty in every day.*

A formula for personal success –

Interest + Goal = Motivation

Motivation + Effort = Success

Success + Achievement = Personal Satisfaction

Personal Satisfaction = Feeling good about one's self

Feeling good about one's self = Happiness and Productivity

Poetry can nourish your soul, renew your spirit, and propel positive actions.

*Persistence means not being deterred
from pursuing your dreams and
goals no matter how pessimistic
the odds-makers may be about your
probability of success.*

Most of us have the ability to think,
speak, and make decisions.
The most important of these is
the ability to think.

*Do not allow anyone to be responsible
for your failure.*

We are "they."

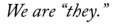

Do not hate anyone. Hate is a threat to your humanity.

*To help set the agenda you must
be at the table. Never trust others
to represent your interests
as well as you can.*

*We must teach our children
the importance of doing well
and doing good.*

*The three greatest gifts that we
can give our children are
teach them to love themselves,
to believe that they can do well,
and to never, ever give up.*

*We can change the world if we do it
one person at a time, beginning
with ourselves.*

Too often consensus means choosing peace over principles.

It is impossible to be burned out if you have never been on fire.

*The wealthiest person in the world is
one who has food, shelter, friends,
and passion for a cause that
improves the human condition.*

Hope is what drives winter from the soul.

Choose to believe that you can make the world better and proceed to do so.

In every challenge there is an opportunity. Our capacity to see the opportunity and to seize it is a matter of our vision and our values.

DREAMS

The only thing larger than your dream should be your imagination.

*Don't let the demons of doubt and fear
rob you of your dreams. We should
be so focused in pursuit of our dreams
that not even our fears and doubts
can survive the strength and
force of our faith.*

Don't let the ism twins –
racism and sexism –
kill your dream.

Dreams are what keep hope alive.
Dreams without hope are only
illusions; dreams are the stuff
that hope is made of.

Aspiration, motivation and preparation are the prerequisites for success in whatever one chooses to do.

*The primary role of parents is to nurture
the dreams of their children.*

*As parents, teachers, and preachers —
indeed all people of goodwill —
we must imbue children with the
belief that dreams can come true if
they have the courage to pursue them.*

*Three-fourths of achieving your dream
entails believing that you can.*

SPIRITUALITY

*Faith is a far more powerful
motivator than fate.*

If we listen carefully enough, we can hear God's voice no matter how noisy the crowd.

We all have a calling but some choose to ignore theirs.

*One can be materially wealthy yet
poverty stricken spiritually.*

We shouldn't insult God by asking Him to do for us that which we can do for ourselves.

God may not have given us the same length of time, but he gave us the same amount of time. How we use that time is up to each of us.

*Too many preachers and religious
teachers are so concerned with
preparing people for life after death
that they do not prepare them
for the hell on earth.*

Armed with a mustard seed of faith, a dash of hope, a pound of persistence and a ton of work, you can set about the task of pursuing your dream.

*Without a permanent fuel source
your light will go out.*

Spirituality is tonic for the soul.

EDUCATION

*Education is more than a
collection of courses.*

Possessing a degree is not the same as being educated. One can be ignorant and degreed at the same time.

Education is the best choice for overcoming poverty, racism and cynicism.

The segregationists of the south realized, as did Civil Rights activists, that education – quality education – wherever it is delivered is a liberator of people and that it prepares them for opportunities.

When it comes to job opportunities, acquiring the desired preparation and experience keeps you from being screened out by an employer.

If the academy is to become more responsive to societal needs generally, and to the needs of people of color in particular, colleges and universities must be led by those who inspire confidence, instill hope and educate students who are committed to Truth, Wisdom and Justice.

*Don't let your education
go to your head.*

*If you have a choice of weapons
for overcoming racism and sexism,
choose education.*

Education is the engine of opportunity. If we let that engine idle millions of people will lose hope.

Service learning and applied research are not new forms of domestic missionary work by those in the academy.

EQUITY/EQUALITY/DIVERSITY

*Equity and excellence are core
principles of democracy and
both are achievable.*

*Equity can be defined broadly enough
to include anyone who has suffered
the effects of discrimination and
disfranchisement.*

Equity without excellence is hollow.

Diversity is not a substitute for equity.

Anyone who uses the system to his advantage without challenging the system to change for the benefit of all disfranchised people is the enemy irrespective of race or social status.

No matter how successful you are, being black means wondering if your son will be shot by a white cop because he "looked like a criminal."

Those who argue that affirmative action stigmatizes African Americans are often the ones who have benefited from affirmative action the most.

Anyone who opposes utilizing all affirmative methods of leveling the playing field for African Americans is in denial about the historical and contemporary effects of enslavement, racism and discrimination.

Screening people in requires creativity and compassion, screening them out is a no-brainer.

*While it's true that not all whites
owned slaves; they all benefited from
the system that supported slavery.
It's called white privilege.*

Racism kills more people than cancer and heart attacks combined. Racism kills the spirit and saps the soul.

*The only person more dangerous than
a racist is the apologist for a racist.*

*Too many people would rather settle
for pay and peace than to challenge
a system that they know is unjust,
corrupt, and bankrupt.*

*We will have a color blind society
when white is no longer right.*

*One of the most powerful people
in the world is one who is willing
to stand up for justice.*

*Poverty is not an excuse for
tolerating injustice.*

*Blacks would have pulled themselves
up by their bootstraps long ago,
but few of us had boots.*

Never laugh at ethnic or sexist jokes
no matter how humorous
they may be to others.

*Too often, diversity has become a
vehicle for allowing many white
people to assuage their guilty conscious
without dealing seriously
with the effects of racism and the
disfranchisement of
black and brown people.*

*Refusing to get out of our comfort zone
is the most significant deterrent to
achieving the diversity that
we vehemently espouse.*

COMPASSION AND COMMITMENT

*Just as faith without works is dead,
commitment without will is a fallacy.*

Not leaving the world better than we found it is an unpardonable sin.

*Never forego the opportunity to use
your voice to speak for the voiceless.*

*Failure is not an option when others
are depending on you.*

One of the best things about changing the world is the fact you don't have to form a committee. You can be a change agent of one.

Freedom is far more than the opportunity to choose where one may live, work, worship, or socialize. Freedom is the obligation to leave the world better than we found it.

*Perhaps the greatest deterrent to
social change is our basic
unwillingness to challenge
the status quo.*

*True people of conscious are those
who are willing to confront
rather than conform.*

*How can we profess to be pro life and
allow one in six children in America
to go to bed hungry every night?*

LEADERSHIP

*Your intellect, energy, and position
should not be used to perfect
the status quo.*

*There is a time to lead and a time
to be led. As agents of change we must
know when to do which.*

*Leadership is vision, values, will,
and passion in action.*

Inspiring hope,
that's the first role of a leader.

It is said that African American leaders must start perfect, and then improve.

Leadership is the art of creating opportunities.

*As a leader, you have an obligation
to bring hope to the hopeless and
help to the helpless. Not doing so
is a dereliction of duty.*

The true leader must be willing to agitate and advocate for the disfranchised, even if it displeases those who employ you or call themselves your friends.

*Leadership is an opportunity for service
rather than personal gain.*

*The most significant challenge facing
our nation, indeed the world,
is a dearth of leadership.*

*The most important assets of a good leader
are integrity and persistence.*

COUNSEL

*Don't confuse your blessings
with being lucky.*

Always conceptualize problems from the perspective of your assets rather than your deficits whether in your personal affairs or in business.

*Don't squander your energy and
intellect by being so angry that you
don't have time to correct the wrongs
that are perpetrated by those
in positions of power.*

The best time to start is NOW.

To succeed requires a combination of readiness, resolve, and resiliency.

*When confronted with a choice
between principles and pay, choose
principles. In the long run your
principles will pay.*

In order to march to the beat of your own drum, you must learn to listen to the music of your heart.

*In order to be effective change agents,
we must be authentic, possess integrity
beyond reproach and commitment
not bound by timeframes.*

All movement is not progress.

You are more than the sum of your material possessions.

*Don't confuse who you are with
what you have or confuse who you are
with what you do.*

*Your work should be an extension
of you, rather than you being an
extension of your work.*

In your decision-making, never substitute doing what is right with what is proper.

Don't wear your true emotions
on your face.

*Don't confuse being educated
with being wise.*

*The loneliest person in the world is the
one who is not comfortable in his
or her own company.*

Never tire of doing good.

*Who you are is more important
than what you are.*

If given the opportunity to change anything in the world you wish to change, always choose yourself.

*Unless you have been in the valley,
you cannot experience the thrill of
being on the mountain top.*

*Before cloning any additional people
we should try to take care of
those already here.*

*There is a difference between being
a male and being a man. All men are
males, but not all males are men.
Being a man is a combination of
gender, attitude, and behavior.
Being male simply refers to the genetic
capacity to procreate or the ability to
produce children. My granddaddy
would have said it this way
"being a man is more than
breath and britches."*

Do something that makes you happy.